IF ONE CONTINUES
TO SURVIVE

An Anthology of Resistances

Curated by

Joshua C. Pipkins with assistance from Angel Rosen

—all proceeds from this project support The Audre Lorde Project—

Querencia Press – Chicago IL

QUERENCIA PRESS

© Copyright 2025

Joshua C. Pipkins

Angel Rosen

Cover art: Chrissy Carlson

ISBN 978 1 963943 47 4

www.querenciapress.com

First Published in 2025

Querencia Press, LLC

Chicago IL

Printed & Bound in the United States of America

"If I didn't define myself for myself, I would be crunched into other people's fantasies for me and eaten alive."

—Audre Lorde

Poetry did not get me through every bad situation. That is not poetry's responsibility. Poetry is a lot like God. It stays with you as a forever ear, but only intervenes when crucial, and when there's no possible way for you to learn from the worst to come. That is when it speaks, its voice comes through you, surges at your fingertips like electricity, and then consumes paper or keyboard. In all that excess of feeling, things become a little more manageable.

The following is a collection of global grievances and resistances...

—Joshua C. Pipkins

CONTENTS

Dào (俳句)

the path I shall take
ripples from within my heart
Towards the future

I trust that no one
knows better than me myself
The way to progress

—Aria Victoria Leadford

Washing The Dishes

Washing the dishes, I greet cardinal birds at my window, red feathers fuel truculence. I drain the orange substance out of mandarin orange cans, and I smile. Washing the dishes, I pick yellow lemon peels from Tupperware my mother swears she won't ever throw away; I guess the nostalgia gives her glee. Green olives perish in the blades of the garbage disposal, their scent amuck, but they still yearn for a new life. Washing the dishes, I smear blue Dawn dish soap on paper plates, I work hard to kill grease, work too hard on such a fragile thing. Indigo pierces through the curtains, night has since blanketed the world but I still stand there in my kitchen, washing the dishes. I'm still washing the dishes and I will keep washing the dishes until you stop leaving dirt in my sink. I wash the dishes until my hands turn purple, bruised knuckles brace for impact with dinner's debris. We eat around the table together, but we're not all there. At least I can wash the dishes when everyone's done.

—**Matthew Brooks**

escalate

i want to live in a world where orange
is the color of faded sunsets, not
despots and the ensuing
state repression—where leaving the house
doesn't require a signal thread,
escalation plan, a mood board
of what would have been. is fascism just

the state of having feared bigotry long enough
that it arises like a malfunction in the normal?
—tried to cower in fear,
then to resist, and either way all i could feel
was the mirage or reality bearing down.
my only project in 2025 is a haphazard
safety plan, a notes-app autobiography
of what's been lost—of two escape plans

at once, a red state and a society as
grey and unforgiving as ice—anti-trans
legislation is just the legitimized version
of the mold i used to shape my body,
of the normal, the cast-iron ideal
her glow of burnt-orange, the perfect
yet still grotesque in the eyes of the free

i didn't eat for a summer and haven't

transitioned enough for a lifetime
will i ever read enough
apologetic think pieces to understand why
cis men would choose another cis man

over disruption? probably,
but that doesn't make it any easier
to turn off the news.

—**mk zariel**

Soft Things

A boy lies alone on a dusty bed,
and he doesn't know when the birds
stopped singing, just that it's noon
and they should still be out.
He thinks about the white room,
porcelain old and porcelain rich,
small enough to be the container
of curious spectacles.
The cabinets are brimming,
little statues and trinkets,
that were once prized,
now only touched
when making space.
The boy opens the big window,
and he thinks, maybe today
is the day, even though
it could be any among the week.
Wondering how he feels
about being here
like a misplaced valuable
used for casual decoration,
and how the bedside table feels
besides being hard all the time,
how outside there are gardeners,

manicured bushes and trees
that remind him
of his job.
The sky is cloudy,
and a storm is on the horizon,
the rain drops reminds him
of the coastlines that belong
to his dreams,
and he extends his tongue,
letting the water
loosen whatever
has thickened in his throat,
and his mouth,
cotton stuffed
in the space
between his gums

and lips.

—**Brandon Shane**

Oyster Girl

—after Danez Smith

oyster girl. oyster curious. walrus hungry.
swallow oyster soup. crack an oyster shell.
oyster girl marching broken along the shore.
coastline gets longer, the shorter her unit of
measure. prophesying like cassandra.
oyster girl follows the mandelbrot curve.
oyster fractal. oyster neuron. she's been
worried about the weather. lightning doesn't
strike in a straight line.
oyster girl. oyster furious. carpenter hungry.
oyster girl is never satisfied.

—**Sai Chi**

A Beautiful Defense

Sitting alone at a table for one
Working through a dish of the inexpressible
I watch the world perform itself and
Chew on the promise of
Freedom
One candle, reflected in the prism of my water glass
thoroughly fails to extinguish the black depths.
Who can see into ocean canyons but slowly, and with the heart?
A school of silvery ideas scuttled by icy rage and circumstance
strike out in every direction,
eyes wide open, and
Lock in on
Freedom
As my beautiful mind helpfully disintegrates,
a private wish, a faint point of light, begins to emerge through
the blackened kitchen
window
even though I can no longer see. Broken shards of my self form
a murmuration that reels and tumbles
In a beautiful defense of
Freedom
Suspended in time
as I crunch on a salad I can no longer hear
Scattershot pieces of my soul begin to unbreak.

A sky, soft and vast, begins

disappears
and reappears, mesmerizing and enchanted,

like a colossus black flower blooming
in timelapse, and
my attention turns
in a
Shuuushhhhuuushhhh
of wings, soft, ragged petals shot through with bone. I am
Trapped in the winds of
Freedom
Swirling heat rises from my soup as I steal precious and careful
sips
of agency.
My intuition provides critical intelligence while covertly
dancing across

the finest of lines to draw strength from my own conclusions.
Relief, the dawning of the impermanence of forever defeats,
whispers WE WILL RISE as
Hundreds of thousands each
FIGHT

our

way

to

Freedom

Black coffee, hot,

is as bitter as any self-respecting medicine.

Raising a cup I take my first sip, triage and treatment, and

Drink to

Freedom

Sitting alone

At a table for one

—**Emily Cross**

Breaking The Box

all of my life
i have tried to make myself
less,
to make everyone else
comfortable;
didn't really realize how small
it made me feel at first—
but now i know
that i have every right to take up
space,
and i have always been worthy;
if people don't like my rainbow
heart then i will simply carry on
without them in my life—
because life is too short to simply
remain in a closet for the comfort of others,
i deserve to be as bright and vibrant
as i am and wish to be with every
hope, thought, prayer, and dream;
and so i will resist anyone who tries to push
me back into the box of who they thought
i was.

—Linda Crate

rant for anti-trans legislation

—after nat raum's "this book will not save you"

this dyke will not be any better at sports than
a teenage boy. nor do i particularly
want to be, because sports are for people who
value competition, and i'm not even
a person. this dyke will not be an enlivening presence
in the public bathroom, not enough
to need quarantining, protection. this dyke has
no need for health, care,
or healthcare. this dyke has pronouns
and is not afraid to use them. this dyke tried
to mount an insurrection against its
elementary school, and every school board
is powerless to stop the anarchy of a trans five-year-old.
this dyke doesn't say gay,
that's far too assimilationist. this dyke has a void on its legal
gender marker &
is the reason public queer performance needs
a legal definition & has no need for respectability.

—mk zariel

YOU JUST HAVE TO FETCH A GROWN-UP, DEAR

"You just have to fetch a grown-up, dear,"
dad told them in year five
When Arnie kicked and Lily spat and
they didn't want to be alive

"You have to pretend it's nothing
and eventually they'll leave you be,"
the teacher said, but Noah still gave
them the finger when no one could see

"And I know that message was horrid,
that sort of thing will not stand
But although he has some issues
he'll grow up to be a fine young man"

"You just have to fetch a grown-up, dear,"
they repeated, earnestly
as everyone kept on talking
and the councillor gave them tea

"You just have to fetch a grown-up, dear,"
they told them again and again
So for years they kept right on fetching
until the assault on their closest friend

That day they acquired a baseball bat
and practised relentlessly

They wrote on it, in capital letters
for everyone to see:

A GROWN-UP

"You just have to fetch a grown-up, dear,
I'm sure it will stop one day."
They thought about this for a second
Then, smiling, they said: "Okay."

—**Thomas Herlofsen**

Courage to Scream

To scream not from fear, but out of
love.
I want to shout your praises until
my throat is scorching.
Words of fire lit by your
excellence.

I will scream, not from love but
fear.

Horrified of a crowd that will rip
me away
    and rip you apart.

To scream out of love, I fear.
A flare it is to scream.
A flare, calling to the horde.

I am a coward, to scream.
But a lion's heart wails
    and a bull's quivers.

I want to give myself to you.
Throw myself at the swarm,
Stingers boiling under my skin.

So, I face forward with stubborn
pride.
Since the world refuses to love us,
I will love us with the strength of
the world.

One day, I will not need to scream.
I whisper softly your praises.
    and that is enough

—**Mars Mittelstadt**

The Cost of Survival

Life is a thing   to be lived rather than survived
              they believed
they said   they believed
       they said from their safeties and their houses and their doctors
       and their henchmen and their happiness of not thinking about
       the next day
                          the next cold
                          the next meal
Their gazes I survived
       all over my face and body and the decisions they thought I made
       something   blue
       out of a scar
       feeling   blue
       my eyes taken from me
       ears bloody with ichor
       skin screaming   the more you gentle
                                      it
They say love is a thing   to be lived
              they believed
          demanded that I see
         with irises taken and misplaced
             it's not the same
             it's not the same

              but I don't want   to be gentled   again
and so I lose

              over

                    and over

                    what could have been

Lose only what you can   spare

I can dance and I may scream

I can hide   in the biggest clothes   money can buy

I can cut the parts that hurt   and find   I'm not smaller

I shall play the part of a bird

                              never

                                    to be held

But I lose again

              even though there is nothing to lose

                                                  but me

              in the first place

              I lose   but not me

              now that there is value

              I lose   but not me

                    for I cannot   see

                                        hear

                                        touch

                                        trust

for I could learn   again

when the world is gentled   but not by me

—Florence Rivières

You are your own mirror

When I was a girl
I used to survive   their eyes
      by giving what they sought
      their ears
      by keeping as quiet   as I could   as I cannot anymore
      images don't need a voice they thought
      a model they called me

I took up   space my arms a corolla   my legs a treat
I took up space   inch
      by inch
      one decibel at a time
      a joke here   some wit there
      until they got so used to it
      even I didn't realize
      I was now speaking
      full sentences

and instead of the woman-child in the boudoir they started portraying other things things that weren't in their mind's eyes they found themselves with a tree-ghost a sea-nymph a savage she-they-wolf a wild child reveling in torrents and dirt and waterfalls

drawing strength from new pictures
of self
drawing the power
to say no

Personality they called it
Singular they called me
unable to see
               we were all alike
                   all models, once rendered free   were people
and they praised and praised and praised
to get me back   in their gaze   where I belonged
you are perfect as you are they said
long hair and breasts and skin blue from cold and love
praised all the lines on my arm
old soul they called me
               some tried to smother the edges
               but only   two
               fragments of flesh
               I wanted gone
               for even then
               I wasn't a girl

and by   then
I was already free.

—**Florence Rivières**

Better for Having Walked With You

Dad used to say, "Walk with a man who limps
and soon, you'll be walking with a limp."
I ignored that thinking, "What of the man with the limp.
Will he walk better for having walked with you?"
That last summer before I went away to school
I worked at the steel plant to make tuition.
Dad didn't tell me, his friend, my supervisor
offered to keep me on working.
My mother swore him to secrecy.
I left for school as planned, it wasn't me
to keep working in the factory.
At the university I listened intently
to my History Professor recite,
"When I say 'Man' keep in mind
'Man' embraces woman." Then he smiled.
I didn't like his smile, knowing it wasn't right.
Don't remember anything else he said
too much old boy talk, undoubtedly now he is dead.
Today, female History Professors are teaching
women their rights instead.
Al must be dead too, my boss at the university
I worked for more tuition in the physical plant
under him. Mild mannered. He liked to drink
and occasionally he'd get angry.

We sometimes had a few at the end of the day.
Al was gay and partnered. Loved Pete
more than wine. His Zen advice to me,
"Drink in moderation, embrace women
and you'll be fine."

—**Frank Beltrano**

Skilled Labor

They say identity is within,
but I see it all over the walls,
hung up like portraits
and placed for everyone
to see.
All day they tell me,
not to let him change my personality,
but they don't see
we're everywhere; the foam mattress,
the Persian carpet stained in red wine
and empty bottles of peroxide,
the many cracked tiles
carefully glued together.
Even down the street,
I can hear my body parts thumping
against the windows,
bedframe pounding
dust out the floor,
and they tell me
that healing takes time
but I'm still trying
to remember
what that means.
The next time I kissed,

was some months later,
and it was an accident,
this new boy
told me not to worry
and that all poisons
come with clocks,
and that rivers
always end up
in a larger body
of water.
I laughed,
what a charlatan,
a beautiful fraud
foreshadowing

my murder,
kill me.

—**Brandon Shane**

Anatomy of the Artist

"My searing soul seems to resonate
with the electric hum of the refrigerator
in our kitchen.
Almost always empty,
but entrenched in the enormous effort
of taking the best care of its contents
like the invitation that I keep sacred and waiting for you
shut away in my creaky, concave chest.
A welcoming hearth within a heart.
All those I've known and loved nestled meekly inside of a space
too vast to hold
anything properly,
but beats much like the persistent percussion
of the moody muscle,
tucked away.
I daydream of us
so often dying or lost,
splitting the cost of a cup of coffee
in a city cafe someday,
because we have experienced enough
grief to know that time is just
a humble house of cards next to a teething toddler.
A construct designed to fail us
posing questions about the pathology of persuasion.

A fleeting film roll
set to its own unique nocturne.
A malicious melody of plastic and metal
echoes endlessly behind me
because my emotional traffic
is gridlocked for miles.
As I saunter down the steaming asphalt
paved with good intentions,
a deliciously maddening cycle,
always to you.
I make such profound promises
like some sort of credible criminal
attempting to evade loneliness
with both ankles sprained."

—**Macon Toney**

Where Respite Lives

A spiraling path I unthinkingly follow toward a crater of fire.
No care for the branches that catch at my arms and legs,
The forest limbs striking at my face.
My feet ache, bruised and cut from the pebbles in my shoes,
But I soldier on, heeding the invisible hands pushing at my back,
the whisper of unseen voices—You have to, you have to, you have to.
The flames are now licking at my toes, smoke coating my throat.
And as I cough and sputter, the inferno draws forth a memory,
a nightmare of years past.
I've been this way before.
I slogged this road long ago,
Forced my way to its inexorable end and plunged into the fires.
The symbology may evoke a phoenix, but I am not that exalted creature.
When I burned, I found no cleansing, no rebirth.
There was no rising from the coals and ashes,
transcendent and glorious, powerfully blazing forth.
I am a human woman and I crawled out, a burnt and broken shell,
blistered and raw,
Gasping, choking on a lungful of—I can't do it anymore.
Here and now, I remember that what doesn't kill you can still fuck you up.
So in this moment, I make a new choice.
I shove away those unseen hands.
Wordlessly, I scream, shutting out the voices that hiss—
You have to, you have to, you have to.

I stumble off the path, crashing through the bracken.

The terrain off the path is rough, but my eyes are fixed ahead,

Where I can see a clear space, hear a rushing of water.

To my shock, nobody chases me, and I break through.

As tears of relief trace lines down my soot-smudged cheeks,

I sink to my knees in soft grass, in a peaceful meadow where respite lives.

I sit beside a cool, refreshing stream, soaking my battered feet in its healing waters.

And I breathe deeply, inhaling a great clean lungful of—I won't do it anymore.

—**Anna McCluskey**

war paint

sitting cornered between frailty and the beast,
starvation laced with the lack of sleep
gaping mouth a soul fled from,
gaping legs
yes, that's what this has become

suffocated under heavy restitutions
strung loosely between limbs
and torn redemptions
lost hopes and failed deities
beautiful glances of atrocities

frozen beneath vessels and veins,
organs and trains commuting
populated chemical connections,
cemented prints of where you've been,
pools wade in history's tracking,
and somehow there's smeared blood
across your dress and your face
a sick sort of war paint
for something you never knew you'd be fighting for

—**Jen Kochis**

SHAME

—after Ambition by Victoria Chang

shame died on august 7, 1989
a long and slow and painful death.
the coroner's report said its ribs were
broken, its body bruised.
i granted its wish for
cremation, and dispersed its ashes
without ceremony but many tears.
pride was shame's sibling,
always wanting to tag along,
they were uneasy with each other and fought
till pride, though injured and wounded,
won the battle. still, shame is always
the underside of pride, a second skin, a ghost
that continues to haunt, even in death
before which
they put electrodes on my mother's head. gave her pills
that made her shake and jumble her words.
she sees things that are not there, and tells me
men are trying to kill her. but i knew
this time, it was the end. another's
love for her had almost made her normal.

but then he died suddenly. she didn't need
a temporary fix. she needed a
permanent solution for she could not
find wholeness and health
in body or in mind on her own
but they let her go
wouldn't keep her more than thirty days.
the only question that remains is:
did she jump or was she pushed?

—Line Dufour

ARRHYTHMIA (FOR I HAVE DIED...)

For I have died a dozen trips.
They push the drug into my vein:
On snowy sheets, a bloody stain
When twice or thrice the needle slips,

Before the probing finds its mark.
A dozen times the beat has...ceased...
A dozen times has leapt! at least,
To ease my pain, to slow my heart.

Oh easeful death—this is thy sting.
For this is not the touch of love;
A giant hand—no velvet glove,
To crush the pulse's fluttering wing.

They push the drug into my vein,
I feel it coursing to my heart.
I feel it stop...I feel it start!
Then like the phoenix, rise again—

And again, again, again, again...

I sing my songs, I make my rhymes;
And now I live a dozen times.

—**Jaz Stutley**

Pills

the first time,   I was running up a runner
slinking down the upstairs staircase
wrinkled and caked in dirt
tripping on the rips and tears on the stairs
slinking up the upstairs staircase
too young, too far, too weak
as if I was dreaming, I swam through molasses
wading through stained fabric
finally stepping on stable floor
I bolted to the bedroom door
jolting my sister awake

I cried to her,
"mom is going to take all of her pills
and fall asleep forever."

my sister rolled over
told me not to worry
"she won't."

and she didn't

the next time,   I was awake and swimming through molasses
wading through liquid air
until I reached the ambulance

47

I had called 911,
"I swallowed all of my pills
and now I will die."
but I lived. I lived. I lived.

—Mars Mittelstadt

Let's Burn Something Down Tonight

Let's burn something down tonight.
Let's find something old,
Something we used to think
We could not survive
Without, something significant. Let's
Set it on fire.
An edifice we marveled at,
Something we looked up to,
Tall and strong, in
Admiration of power,
Importance, and potency.
Something we knew was forever,
Now, wondering
Why we ever thought
We couldn't do without it?
Let's burn it down.
Let's set fire to something
That used to be the foundation of
Our being. Something
That would never occur to us
Could sink, erode,
Decay beneath us,
Leave our feet with no solid ground.

Something we built our entire lives on
But fell away. Let's watch what's built on it
List and lean,
Topple and crash by our own hand
Instead of the slow destruction of
Sand and rust.
We can be our own gods,
And end it with our own hands.
Let's burn it down.

—**Adam Tritt**

A Toast To All The Words That Never Made It

Raise your glass to whatever adjective that slipped through the
cracks of our modern languages,
And whatever feeling never got its tale.

To all the grammatical rules and 6th or 7th conjugations that
never got be,
So many words left unsaid that never made the final cut for our
books.

All the terms and phrases that we can't even begin to imagine,
And the congruence with branches, crosses and combinations
we've never seen before.

Sentences structured like nothing the imagination could even
begin to ponder,
With their own rule breakers in little letters.

For every day that lacks a word to describe it,
And every sound that deserved its own.
To every action that got shoved under the label of another.

All the words we never got to make,
And never got put to use.

Cheers.

—**Mika E. Houen**

Sap

"Tell all the Truth but tell it slant— / Success in Circuit lies... /
The Truth must dazzle gradually / Or every man be blind"
—*Emily Dickinson*

Flash! Bam! Alacazam! That's what it feels like to fall in love.
Like a clearcutting blade shaving pine trees off of a mountain
slope, four at time, uprooting them dendrites and all, so that the
soil holds only straggling follicles of what once was fir,
redwood, moss.

Falling slowly—telling the Truth with a slant—is more
meticulous. It's studying each redwood with its soft bark, its red
twined tendrils like soft uncut chin fuzz, and caressing swaths
of it. Removing a tree, piece by piece, soft piece of trunk after
soft piece of trunk. Undressing the tree, falling slowly, allowing
its cleaves to tell You where to go.

Is the tree you, or is it your beloved? Perhaps it's both of you.
The risk of falling slowly—of dazzling gradually—is that you
might reach sap. And if you do, the tree is telling you that
there's a wound there. Sap collects, oozes, gelatinizes where
things have gone awry, astray. If you hit sap, look at with soft
eyes and touch it softly, with the sensitive ridges of your
fingerpads. Touch it, let it leave its trace, its stinging pine scent,

on your hand because, inevitably, glue that it is, sap leaves its mark on you.

—**Sam Pauley**

MY FAT BODY'S FINAL APOLOGY

is in a language you haven't learned yet.
You can't even stomach hearing such a thing.
There is no such thing as a small God,
and nobody worth praying to
is immune to Diet Coke.
You [hold][harbor]
your opinions about my fat body,
until I tell you it's recovered.
Then it's a celebration:
You Survived Thinness!
—reads the store-bought congratulations card,
and I smile sweetly
at your hand-me-down gesture
in between bites of the [sweetest] cake
I've ever had.
My fat body's final apology
was a service rendered on a Tuesday,
friends/family being received
between the hours of 11 and 2;
a polite amount of time
to be considered,
or remembered,
or heard.

My fat body's final apology
is available as an Audiobook
for free if you subscribe.
In between the ad breaks,
you can hear me scream.

—**Angel Rosen**

We Are Always on Schedule for the Night Shift

We are always on schedule for the night shift.
Our phones stay ready for the call to action.
Our cars stay fueled for a moment's notice.
Our coats and keys stay by the front door.
We are always on schedule for the night shift.
We keep energy drinks to remain awake.
We keep phone chargers to remain connected.
We keep cash to remain in the game.
We are always on schedule for the night shift.
Open couches to share a moment's respite.
Clean clothes to share a fleeting warmth.
Instant meals to share a quick comfort.
We are always on schedule for the night shift.
For a coworker, who looks for a helping hand.
For a friend, who needs a shoulder to lean on.
For a lover, who wishes to be comforted.
We don't know when we will receive the call.
We remain ready for the night we do.
We pray to a god that the call never comes.
We are always on schedule for the night shift.

—**Brett Voloshin**

On Simplicity

There is a certain nuance
that comes with simplicity
That most people rate
as difficulty
But the real difficulty
is to stop adjourning and resisting and instead
Adorning that which needs it most

—**Avital Rimon**

SOMEONE PUT ME ON THE LIST

Someone put me on the list of
those with soft pillows
Someone put me on the list of
those not lying in the ruins
Someone blindly clutched at
my straw, threading wild
strawberries on it
Sometimes, alone
I am ungrateful

—Thomas Herlofsen

Forbidden fruit

Bitter raw fruit ripped
Fresh off the earth
Core dripping white
Overfull with the
Poison I see, yet imbibe
All the same
I've no taste for the morsel,
For the timid glimpse
Lips agape, I claim
Life by the mouthful
Immoderate, ever
Ravenous for
The unbridled giving and
The wanton taking
I'll drown in the shallow, delve
In the crimson depths
Between a lover's thighs
And resurface, all hunger
Restored,
For such is the sap
Upon which I thrive.

—Sofia Lopes

One Mistake I'll Never Make

I learned to fly by trial and error. Now I get so high the Yeomans mistake me for a Tower raven soaring toward Fiddler's Green. But it's no wander-lusting sailor that vexes me like the wind-chilled girl in the sepulcher. Instead, my reason for splitting from the papacy is a matryoshka twirling around on a ruby red music box. Around and around she goes. Where she stops...The ferryman knows her blue-raspberry lips. He tells me there's a charge, a large charge for his service, then points in her direction without acknowledging my copper coins. I always find her house-bound. Trapped beneath scaffolding laid by salt-crusted scarecrows. With forensic precision, I excavate her wooden pieces before storing them all in a velvet sack. Atlas-burden now settled, I prepare for ascent. Ghostflowers swirl past as Eurydice reminds me, don't look back.

—Sai Chi

Thirst

In this sweltering heat
Underneath a blistering sky
We melt, we meld together
And in the drought of the
Years, we thrive, we create
Balmy dewdrops, a shelter
Unto ourselves
Seabound, earthmade—
Water from the skies,
We collapse and rise anew.

—**Sofia Lopes**

EMPTY

I was walking down a lonely road,
Avoiding the crowds, forgetting the pain.
How come I feel so empty inside?

On my journey from the darkness—
What if I hadn't come to that place?
Just questions without answers.

Next to you (during amnesiac times),
While millions are watching the crime.
There ain't no true or false belief.

Just mighty walls of fire,
Peal of laughter the eternal sound...

—**Roger Sandega**

Plenary

Skyping us from
Africa at midnight
a soft-spoken man with
light in his eyes
fills the room with his
incongruous bright smile
he brings us news
from the diamond mines
blood and oil
spilt in the Niger delta
activists face down
shot in the back

platinum miners
striking with shovels
for ten dollars a day
police with riot shields
thirty dead;
the newspapers said five
the latest tactic
is for women to plant gardens
on ancestral land

while elders learn the
words for trespass from

multinational oil companies
thus far it has proved hard
to shift these mothers, aunts,
and matriarchs

standing their ground
with digging sticks
carrying babies on their hips
eighty percent of the world's gold
is sold for women's jewelry
last time he was held
for forty days
no charge, no trial
bruised eyes
broken nose
family in hiding

the circuits short
screens go dark
but we can still hear him

quietly changing the world
from his bedroom

behind him
on a whitewashed wall
pale blue curtains

keep out the night with
small pink flowers.

—**Amanda Hunt**

White Pine

I am the roots of this place

You had some too

But you chopped them off

To plant your feeble flag on pristine land

You laugh as we burn

No different than day one

I shed tears of dew

For those who receive your axe

For your splintered core

But you misunderstand each drop

You don't have ownership

This far from your foundation

These trees ignite but they regrow

With time and tears

I'll step out of the white pine

Like my ancestors did

I'll turn into stone and remain

As the earth shifts

Again

Again

You

Baseless

Will cling to your gilded banister

Hold on to your good book as the last page disappears

Wander your labyrinth as prey
Or monster
Your titles won't save you this far from home
Disoriented skeleton

532 years feels significant to the lost
But first people are perennial

—Amanda WouldGo

Sorrow Of The Streets

The children of the soul escape in the streets
Cries echoing out to those who are hollow
Raindrops of discord wail through the villages

The memories of birth hurt before dawn
The seasons of tears escape in the streets
Dreamers mourn in the streets
Harmony slipping through their fingers

Death Xòe's around the men
The spotlight slowly fading
Curtains drawing to a close

Mothers join the snowflakes in stillness
Dressed in the colours of a gloom imagination

—**Kaiana Danning**

Theatre Talks

i know a man in a war

he knew a man in a war

who never came back to say hello

hello

he says each morning

before the sun comes up

he sips his tea

eats his ramen

draws his animals

hello

i sip my coffee

eat my toast

write my stories

we don't talk about

but acknowledge

the hours between us

the dark possibility

i want to be somewhere else

wouldn't it be nice

to not be scared to

but eager to live?

yeah...

fifteen hours later.

that would be nice.

—**Joshua C. Pipkins**

Abuse St.

Everything here is barren
And all cold.

Desperation fills the cracks
Of all the mistreatment
That had happened to these homes.

The abuse of alcohol and drugs
Fills the hollow, desolate neighborhood.

The streets filled with blood,
Blood that had stained here
For all of the road's years.

The abuse that lies near this street,
The absence of safety and trust.

The pain that haunts the homes.
The echoes of the terrible events,
A distant lullaby to be heard.

Abuse street is my home,
It's where I lived my whole life.

Through all the urban legends
That lay with its history,
None that speak the truth.

This street is no man's land.
No one truly knows what happened.

The events that repeat themselves,
The ponds being filled with pollution.
Urbanization wants to forget this street.

It's failed through the generations,
No one wants to be on this street.

Through all the abuse here
To the truth being sifted,
I know the truth of this street.

The truth that no one even knows.
The truth that abuse does not want out...

Only I can know the truth.

—**Quivon Syvoravong**

TAP/TAMP

When you decide to leave
The greatest thing you have ever known,
They try their best to prepare you for the rest.
But you will know it as TAP and TAMS.
You spend a week in a neat little room,
Sitting in neat little rows and wearing less neat suits,
Trying to learn about a life that is alien to you.

Polish your resume, but soften it too.
No one wants to know
What sound a round makes
As it screams over your head.
Depending on who you ask,
It may first whistle, hiss, or sing,
Before it cracks or snaps
Like a little bolt of lightning
Meant only for you.

- Performs well under pressure.

No one wants to hear
How your Marine is haunted
With the memory of those he killed
Or how he tries to kill them again

By drowning his soul in booze.
How can he be indomitable
When you sat up in his room
All night. You listened to his stories
And his sobs, but were unable to comfort him.

- Strong leadership skills.

If the resume isn't for you, college is a fine choice too.
A word of advice for lecture halls:
Sit where you can see all the doors,
Because the only way to stand a room
With 200 strangers is to watch
Their hands and faces as they enter.
Otherwise you'll not hear the lecture.
Only feel hungry eyes probing
In the back of your skull for weakness.

Campus will feel just as alien
As those first days of Afghanistan,
And the culture of your classmates
As bewildering as any tribal custom.
You may scoff at how many of them walk
With heads bowed from the strain

Of living through their phones.
Yet you may find that phone irresistible—
A siren call offering escape from uncertainty.

In a week you will learn so much and so little,
But two things will be clear as day.
This life is now over and closed to you,
And no leader will be there to guide you through.
But remember who you are in the days ahead,
You have weathered trials worse than this,
And this new life will not get the best of you.

—Matthew Keillor

Black Rice

You drank, drank until stooped,
you sat hovering,
mumbling unintelligibly
devouring black rice,
rice that on other occasions
would be called wild and delicious.
"Delicious" you say, momentarily
being intelligible but
then again the mumbling.
And I wonder what you taste
taste after glass upon
glass of white wine until

your mouth is the half-
dead opening of the half-
dead body intoxicated

to the point of fitful
mumbling sleep.
Someone has taken down
the black wire crucifix
put Christ upside down
in the other room,
on the window ledge,

the sun sets behind Him.
Earlier, while you were
more lucid, crows came,
crows came as the sun set,
and the wild poets gathered
to share the words
of the dead.
Tonight, you have sacrificed
yourself to drink and black rice
mumbling until
you rise, take a half-empty bottle of wine
a half-full glass of wine and
your disgust with my appeal for restraint,
you rise, take your half-dead body to sleep
perhaps one or two more
sloshes of death before
you go, and I know
this is not good.
I have been you.

—**Frank Beltrano**

At One

Sometimes I stare
Through windows
Late at night
I'm marvelling
At all the gleaming lights I see
And all the sound of life outside
Right there
And all the gloomy darkness
And imploding silence
On the inside
Here
With me
It's then
I hold the pitch-black murkiness at bay
With my bare hands
Not even a glance
I can feel it tear
At the borders of reality
While I
Sit still
So still
I am taking my chance at sheer will
If I'm closing my eyes tightly
I can see a ray

Of sunshine

Breaking through eternity

Sometimes I stand

Out at the shore

At night

I'm marvelling

At all the living things inside

The sea

And all the dead ones

At the glimmering movement

Of the band of light

That runs

Inbetween

Above and below

With the tide

It's then

I feel the beauty in the darkness of the sea

And the tugging of the water

And the longing to be free

I can sense a sharp wind blowing

And the sand between my toes

Midnight purple clouds are brewing

Strong gales setting sails to woes

While I

Stand still

So still

Like a rock in the surge

I will

Weather the storm

I will greet being torn

Apart

Like a lover

I urge it on still

It's the same wind that will

Be blowing the cover

Of clouds

On its way

To be reborn

Again

Sometimes I lie still

Late at night

I'm marvelling

At feeling like a million particles of light

Making one whole

And darkness

As an old friend

Passes through

Like an eclipse
Not an apocalypse
I'm breaking moonlight on eternal waves
I am the shimmering band of light
Just inbetween above and down below
I am reflecting light and night alike
And with the rise and falling of the tide
I flow

—Mika Rain

ANTHEM

Strike while the spirit's hot.
Strike when the bright blood wills.
Strike to expunge the rot—
it cleanses as it kills.

Strike with the knife, the axe:
hewing the speech that bites.
Strike with the pen, the facts.
Rage is a tool for rights.

Strike while your banners fly
earning your purpose here;
shout witness to the sky,
let it be free and clear.

Strike, hearts joined in the fray:
one creature, voice and tongue
flooding the narrow way,
age standing by the young.

Strike tinder with the light.
Fuel anger with the flame.
Life is a fight or flight.
Strike! I will do the same.

—**Jaz Stutley**

ABOUT THE CONTRIBUTORS

❖ **Joshua C. Pipkins** is a Pushcart-nominated poet based in Memphis, Tennessee. They are the author of *The Flag of Versailles* and *A Quiet God Howling Over Hymns.*

❖ **Angel Rosen** (she/her) is a poet based in a small town near Pittsburgh. She is passionate about friendship, musicals, and mental health. Angel is the recipient of the 2025 Maureen Seaton Poetry Prize. Her work has been published by *Rogue Agent, HAD, Thimble, Roi Fainéant Press,* and others. Befriend her at angelrosen.com.

❖ **Frank Beltrano** (he/him) has been a member of the dynamic poetry community of London, Ontario, Canada. Now living in Lévis, Quebec he founded the poetry group, Strong Threads. He is published in *Carousel, Geist, Beliveau Review, in Canada, Fledgling Rag, US1 Worksheets, Moonstone Press,* and *Rattle Magazine* in the US.

❖ **Matthew Brooks** (he/him/his) is a poet based in Memphis, Tennessee. His strong suits are queer poetry that interrogates sexuality in the obscure realm. His chapbook "Leave it on the Kitchen Table" explores sexuality through the use of metaphors from common kitchen appliances and food items. He studied Creative Writing at the University of Memphis.

❖ **Sai Chi** (she/they) is a writer and multimedia artist living near Orlando, Florida. They are currently studying Creative Writing at the University of Central Florida.

❖ **Linda M. Crate** (she/her) is a Pennsylvanian writer whose poetry, short stories, articles, and reviews have been published in a myriad of magazines both online and in print. She has twelve published chapbooks the latest being: *Searching Stained Glass Windows For An Answer* (Alien Buddha Publishing, December 2022).

❖ **Emily L. Cross** (she/her) is a writer, photographer, and engineer based in Shelburne, Vermont. She is currently reading science fiction short stories and exploring poetry and songwriting.

❖ **Kaiana Danning** (they/them) is an aspiring human rights lawyer. Getting a BA in law and criminology, they write poems for hobbies and are focused on real life issues.

❖ **Line Dufour** (she/her) graduated with a Masters in Creative Writing and Critical Thinking from the University of Gloucestershire and her poems have been included in literary magazines and anthologies.

❖ **Thomas Herlofsen** (he/him) is a Norwegian writer and musician. His most prevalent English language work is the song *Later You Told Me*, recorded and co-created by Amanda Palmer. He lives in Skien, Norway.

❖ **Mika E. Houen** (she/her) is a social science and math student currently living in Denmark. She writes poetry and other forms of fiction as a hobby in her spare time.

❖ **Amanda Hunt** (she/her) is an Aotearoa New Zealand poet and environmental scientist. Her work has been published in *Landfall,*

Poetry NZ, *takahē* and many other New Zealand journals and anthologies. In 2016 she was shortlisted for the Sarah Broom Poetry Prize.

❖ **Matthew R. Keillor** (he/him) is a writer and Marine veteran in Houston, Texas. He has a bachelor's degree in journalism from Texas State University.

❖ **Jen Kochis** (she/her) loves to write in her free time in an effort to make sense of a very nonsensical world. When no one listens, she writes.

❖ **Aria V. Leadford** (they/them) is a writer and artist, currently in their final year of Creative Writing at University of Memphis, who also writes haiku and tanka poems.

❖ **Sofia Lopes** (she/her) is a Brazilian poet, writer, and translator. She holds an MA in Literature and Social Practices, and is currently working towards a PhD focused on literature, technology, and interactive fiction.

❖ **Anna McCluskey** (she/her) is an Oregon-based, semi-nomadic, almost-entirely-feral travel blogger, fantasy author, and poet.

❖ **Mars Mittelstadt** (he/they) is an aspiring poet based in South Central Wisconsin. They are studying Creative Writing at the University of Wisconsin - Madison.

❖ **Sam Pauley** ("SPA") uses they/them pronouns and strives for a world where everyone belongs. They have been published under the name Sam Allen in *Center of Attention: Poems on Stockton & San*

Joaquin (Tuleburg Press) and in Bell Press' 2023 *Poetry Plans*. They are a Master's of Psychology Student at Alliant International University, studying to become a therapist. They live in Northern California with a rambunctious cat named Scout. You can access their content at https://bit.ly/4aW0Ua2.

❖ **Mika Rain** (she/her, they/them) is a neuroqueer AuDHD writer and performer from Germany living in Ireland. She is currently rebuilding life following an autistic burnout and late diagnosis. She has not yet made it to any of the Socials.

❖ **Avital Rimon** (she/her) is a Brooklyn-based storyteller who leans into reflexive narrative in both writing and multimedia art. Her practice often integrates drawing, audio, and personal archives to produce accessible interactive installations or rituals. More at https://ko-fi.com/avitalmediam.

❖ **Florence Rivières** (they/them) is a French writer and poet. They also write for games and comics and can usually be found hitchhiking or brewing tea.

❖ **Roger Sandega**, born 1977 in Vienna, Austria, writes short stories in German as well as poems in German, English & sometimes Spanish. Other interests are photography & painting. Working at a theatre, but not on stage...

❖ **Brandon Shane** (he/him) is a Pushcart and BOTN-nominated poet and horticulturist, born in Yokosuka, Japan. You can see his work in *trampset, The Chiron Review, IceFloe Press, The Argyle Literary*

Magazine, among others. He graduated from LBCC with an English degree.

- **Jaz Stutley** (she/her) holds a B.A. in Writing and Literature, an Associate Diploma of Editing, and a Graduate Diploma of Children's Literature. She is based in regional Victoria, Australia. She has worked in Educational Publishing for nearly twenty years: assessing manuscripts, writing and editing fiction, non-fiction, and fantasy texts for Primary School Literacy projects, including for *National Geographic*. Her other writing includes published poetry, song lyrics, and short stories for adults.

- **Quivon J. Syvoravong** (he/him) is a recent author in high school based in Winfield, Kansas. Quivon has been writing poems and short stories since 2022 and plans to release a full-length poetry collection in the near future.

- **Macon Toney** (they/them) is a poet and tech enthusiast hailing from Florence, South Carolina. They are currently self-studying web design in addition to writing poetry in their down time.

- **Adam Byrn Tritt** (he/him) is an award winning poet and essayist. He is an activist and educator, as well as the founding director of Foundation 451, getting banned books to the communities who need them. He lives in Chisholm, Minnesota.

- **Brett Voloshin** (he/him) is a rising poet based in Eastern Pennsylvania, who values the freedom to express oneself despite the opinion of others.

❖ **Amanda WouldGo** (she/they) is a Wampanoag and Secwepemc artist and writer living in California. She is a 2023/2024 animation and screenwriting fellow with the Native American Media Alliance and is currently working on her first graphic novel.

❖ **mk zariel** {it/its + masc terms} is a transmasculine neuroqueer poet, theater artist, movement journalist, and BashBack aligned anarchist. it is fueled by folk-punk, Emma Goldman, and existential dread. the author of *VOIDGAZING* (2026, Whittle Micropress) and *BOY APPARITION* (2025, Vinegar Press), it can be found online at https://mkzariel.carrd.co/, creating conflictually queer-anarchic spaces, writing columns for *Asymptote* and *The Anarchist Review of Books*, and being mildly feral in the great lakes region. it is kinda gay ngl.

LGBTQIA+ Resources

The Audre Lorde Project Programs: https://alp.org/programs

The Trevor Project Crisis Hotline:
https://www.thetrevorproject.org/get-help/

ALT Mental Health Resources

Veteran Crisis Line: https://www.veteranscrisisline.net/

Have questions about helping your community during these times?
Check the web for local private-owned organizations committed to the
causes you're interested in. It's more important than ever to put words
into specific action!

"I have come to believe over and over again that what is most important to me must be spoken, made verbal and shared, even at the risk of having it bruised or misunderstood."

—Audre Lorde